Nothing But the Best- A Call to Excellence

All scripture quotations are from the King James Version of the Bible.

Nothing But the Best—A Call to Excellence by Joy Haney

Radiant Life Publications, Stockton, California

First printing, September 1996

ISBN No. 1-880969-23-8

Printed in the United States of America.

TABLE OF CONTENTS

PREFACE

May the Holy Spirit use this book to tap you on the shoulder and nudge you to reach for excellence in the things of God. If your life has lost the glow of the Spirit or the fiery zeal of the early Christians, or if you have settled down into complacency and are giving less than your best, this book is for you.

Someone once said, "The descent to hell is easy."

An unknown sinner who finally found himself, penned these words:

> I lived for myself, I thought for myself,
> For myself, and none beside—
> Just as if Jesus had never lived,
> As if He had never died.

If you have slipped into a rut and are following the road of least resistance, or if you habitually do the things you find least satisfying and if your habits enslave you to a selfish life, those chains can be broken. Samuel Johnson was correct when he penned the following words: "The chains of habit are generally too small to be felt until they are too strong to be broken. Habits are at first cobwebs—at last cables." God can help you break any chain or cable. You can live the abundant life in Christ, giving your best to the kingdom of God and showing forth Christ to the world. You choose your destiny.

To every man there openeth
A Way, and Ways, and a Way,
And the High Soul climbs the High Way,
And the Low Soul gropes the Low,
And in between, on the misty flats,
The rest drift to and fro,
But to every man there openeth
A High Way and a Low.
And every man decideth
The way his soul shall go.

John Oxenham [1]

In your quest for excellence do not be dismayed if you are besieged by trouble, for often those who suffer most have most to give. Do not despair, for many times suffering and trouble are only the forerunners to greater things. Mr. M.R. DeHann wrote the following:

Out of the presses of pain,

Cometh the soul's best wine;
And the eyes that have shed no rain,
Can shed but little shine. [2]

The purpose of this book is to awaken you to a new dedication to Jesus Christ and cause you to be filled with passion towards His cause. Do not settle for less when you are surrounded daily by His great majesty. Rosalee Mills Appleby wrote,

> Every mountain tells of his majesty and every crystal stream reminds us of the Water of life. Each flower that opens pays homage to the Rose of Sharon and the Lily of the valley. His name is written in the splendor all about us and his voice is heard in the song of the robin or redbird as each new spring arrives. His glory is told in the fragrance of the jasmine and jonquil. The eagle on wing is a reminder of the heights to which we are invited. The music of the tossing waves and their pause at twilight are part of his orchestra. [3]

The glory of the Lord is ever present, but we must look towards it, acknowledge Him, and lift our eyes up from that which paralyzes our good intentions and pure motives. God is ever trying to bring abundant life to His children. Although He gives so much to His children, He expects and requires back from them their whole heart.

God is a God of mercy, love, and understanding, but His blessings are upon those that love Him. He will not always tolerate wickedness, lukewarmness, or half-heartedness. He will not accept anything less than our best. He is a jealous God and will not sit on the throne with any other god. The following Scriptures show that He is for those that love Him with all their hearts, but He is against those that continually ignore Him.

- "The Lord preserveth all them that love him: but all the wicked will he destroy" (Psalm 145:20).
- "The Lord is far from the wicked: but he heareth the prayer of the righteous" (Proverbs 14:29).
- "Seek good, and not evil, that ye may live: and so the Lord, the God of hosts, shall be with you" (Amos 5:14).
- "Thus saith the Lord of hosts, the God of Israel; Behold, I will bring upon this city and upon all her towns all the evil that I have pronounced against it, because they have hardened their necks, that they might not hear my words" (Jeremiah 19:15).
- "But know that the Lord hath set apart him that is godly for himself: the Lord will hear when I call unto him" (Psalm 4:3).
- "For thou, Lord, wilt bless the righteous; with favour wilt thou compass him as with a shield" (Psalm 5:12).
- "The Lord rewarded me according to my righteousness; according to the cleanness of my hands hath he recompensed me" (Psalm 18:20).
- "Because they regard not the works of the Lord, nor the operation of his hands, he shall destroy them, and not build them up" (Psalm 28:5).

- "The Lord preserveth all them that love him: but all the wicked will he destroy" (Psalm 145:20).

Why live at odds with God? Why not seek to give your best to Him and to attain excellence? It is not as hard as some think. Sir Joshua Reynolds, one of the most distinguished painters of his day, was asked how he attained to such excellence. He replied, "By observing one simple rule...to make each painting the best." [4]

If you will give each minute your best, all the minutes together will multiply into a day. Each day will be your own original painting, colored by your desire for excellence.

INTRODUCTION

God will not tolerate shortcuts, less-than-the-best performances, or shoddy ways. He is calling the Church to excellence. He once winked at ignorance, but now He is commanding all men and women to repent and live holy lives. He does not overlook sin or allow it to go unpunished. Although He is gentle, kind and longsuffering, and will woo the offender with His love, He still operates His kingdom according to *His* standards, weights and balances.

He smiles upon those who are honestly trying to give their best to Him, but He looks with disapproval upon those who are willfully or stubbornly going against what He has spoken.

In the book of Jeremiah, the Lord pointed out several things that brought His displeasure and judgment. He let His people know that He would not accept their sacrifices because of their pride and sins. "To what purpose cometh there to me incense from Sheba, and the sweet cane from a far country? your burnt offerings are not acceptable, nor your sacrifices sweet unto me" (Jeremiah 6:20).

What were they doing that caused God to say this? He described them in Jeremiah 5:11 as having dealt treacherously against Him, and that they knew not the way of the Lord. God was very descriptive in His disgust with their sin of adultery. Jeremiah 5:7-8 says, "...they then committed adultery, and assembled themselves by troops in the harlot's house. They were as fed horses in the morning: everyone neighed after his neighbor's wife."

Not only did they commit acts of immorality, but they treated God like a liar and contradicted His Word. The people's disregard for God and their disrespect for His prophets and His Word displeased Him immensely. Jeremiah 5:12-13 says, "They have belied the Lord, and said, It is not he; neither shall evil come upon us; neither shall we see sword nor famine: And the prophets shall become wind, and the word is not in them."

Can you imagine people that were called by His name, calling the prophets mere *windbags* and denying God? Because of their attitude, God promised them that they would be destroyed. He said, "Because ye speak this word, behold, I will make my words in thy mouth fire, and this people wood, and it shall devour them" (Jeremiah 5:14). He also told them that nations would come against them and that mighty men would eat up their harvest, flocks, vines and fig trees.

God was disgusted with their rebellion and their lack of fear for Him. The deceit of their wicked, false rulers enraged Him. He criticized the poor way they handled the care of the fatherless and the needy (Jeremiah 5:23-29).

God said He was tired and weary of holding within Him His fury towards them (Jeremiah 6:11). He was sick of their covetousness and the falseness of the prophet who spoke things that were not true, and their lack of blushing and their unashamedness of their sin (Jeremiah 6:13-15).

He told them to go back to their original humility and walk in the old paths of honesty and respect, and to adhere to the Word of God. Jeremiah 6:16 says,

> Thus saith the Lord, Stand ye in the ways, and see, and ask for the old paths, where is the good way, and walk therein, and ye shall find rest for your souls. But they said, We will not walk therein.

In spite of their stubbornness He still gave them hope, and chance after chance to make things right. He said in Jeremiah 7:3, "Thus saith the Lord of hosts, the God of Israel, Amend your ways and your doings, and I will cause you to dwell in this place."

He told them to amend their ways in the following five areas:

1. Oppress not the stranger, fatherless and the widow.
2. Shed not innocent blood.
3. Walk not after other gods.
4. Do not steal, murder and commit adultery.
5. Do not swear falsely.

He then made them a promise: "...Obey my voice, and I will be your God, and ye shall be my people: and walk ye in all the ways that I have commanded you, that it may be well unto you" (Jeremiah 7:23). However, they were stubborn in their own thinking. "But they hearkened not, nor inclined their ear, but walked in the counsels and in the imagination of their evil heart, and went backward, and not forward" (Jeremiah 7:24).

The saddest thing of all is that they would not repent. At one point during His dealings with Israel He basically said, "You would not listen to me so I will not listen to you" (Jeremiah 7:16). Those were cold words from a loving God. He promised that He would bring evil upon them because they walked in their own way and would not heed the law of God.

God has not changed. He requires the same standard of excellency in moral purity, cleanness of heart, and godly principle that He has always required. His blessings are with those who follow after His way.

Paul instructed the Christians that God was not pleased with many of the Israelites that followed Moses because of their actions. "But with many of them God was not well pleased; for they were overthrown in the wilderness" (I Corinthians 10:5). The things that displeased God then were the same things that displease Him now and are listed in I Corinthians 10:6-11: Idolatry, fornication, tempting Christ and murmuring. He sums up the scenario in verse 21: "Ye cannot drink the cup of the Lord, and the cup of devils: ye cannot be partakers of the Lord's table, and of the table of devils."

There is a separating line between God's approval and disapproval. He desires for His people to be holy, to have excellent spirits, and to give Him their whole heart and their best.

AUTHOR'S NOTE

Each of the following chapters begins with the word *Give*. A gift given without love is as cold as a business deal. The message of this book is *LOVE*. The heart must be on fire first with love towards God, then humanity and life itself. Giving is an empty procedure if not done in love. Life must pulsate with love and then the *best* will really be the best.

It is essential for everyone to guard their heart against negative emotions, for if they allow these emotions to dwell inside, they will surely be destroyed and the sweet nectar of life will be subtracted from them. Henry Wadsworth Longfellow penned this truth in strong language as the following poem demonstrates:

> The sole thing I hate is Hate;
> For Hate is death; and Love is life,
> A peace, a splendor from above;
> And Hate, a never ending strife,
> A smoke, a blackness from the abyss
> Where unclean serpents coil and hiss!
> Love is the Holy Ghost within;
> Hate the unpardonable sin!
> Who preaches otherwise than this
> Betrays his Master with a kiss! [1]

I wish to emphasize the portion of the poem which says, *"Love is life."* Words penned over 2,000 years ago are still true today: "...the greatest of these is charity [love]" (I Corinthians 13:13).

"Let us hear the conclusion of the whole matter: Fear God, and keep his commandments; for this is the whole duty of man."

Ecclesiastes 12:13

CHAPTER 1

GIVE YOUR BEST TO GOD

Leftovers are such humble things,
We would not serve them to a guest,
And yet we serve them to our Lord
Who deserves the very best.

We give to Him leftover time
Stray minutes here and there,
Leftover cash we give to Him,
Such few coins as we can spare.

We give our youth unto the world,
To hatred, lust and strife;

Then in declining years we give
To Him the remnant of our life.

Author unknown [1]

Leftovers are unacceptable to God. He has a standard of excellence for His people, and He desires them to live up to it. From the beginning of time, God required something of His people.

Imprinted deeply into the minds of the teeming Israeli people was God's law, which required the *best* of everything offered unto Him. When King Saul disobeyed the command of Samuel the prophet and kept back part of the sheep during the battle against the Amalekites, he used the aged law to help justify what he had done. "And Saul said, They have brought them from the Amalekites: for the people spared the *best* of the sheep and of the oxen, to sacrifice unto the Lord thy God" (I Samuel 15:15). Even though the act was wrong, they were operating on the principle of the long-ingrained law of their people: the best animals were offered for sacrifice unto the Lord.

They were also aware that governors, kings, and royalty were worthy of the best. When there was a famine in the land of Canaan, Jacob heard that there was corn in Egypt and sent his sons down to buy some for their families. Upon returning, they discovered in the sacks the money they had paid for the corn. When this corn ran out, Jacob again sent his sons to Egypt to buy more corn. Notice the way he planned to approach the governor:

> And their father Israel said unto them, If it must be so now, do this; take of the best fruits in the land in your vessels, and carry down the man a present, a little balm, and a little honey, spices, and myrrh, nuts, and almonds (Genesis 43:11).

The ancient people that were separated unto God operated on the old established custom of giving God the best for sacrifice, and were reminded from time to time that God walked among them.

> For the Lord thy God walketh in the midst of thy camp, to deliver thee, and to give up thine enemies before thee: therefore shall thy camp be holy: that he see no unclean thing in thee, and turn away from thee (Deuteronomy 23:14).

Just as God walked among them, so He walks among us today.

This book is to remind you that even though God's laws have changed from the time of the Old Testament to the New Testament, His requirements have not changed. He still requires the best from each of us. This book is a call to excellence. In these last days, "Therefore let us not sleep, as do others; but let us watch and be sober" (I Thessalonians 5:6). "See then that we walk circumspectly, not as fools, but as wise, Redeeming the time, because the days are evil" (Ephesians 5:15).

In the closing days of this dispensation it is time to cleanse our hearts, purify our minds, and simplify our lives. It is time to get rid of some things that would keep our feet on the ground instead of meeting Jesus in the clouds.

> For the Lord himself shall descend from heaven with a shout, with the voice of the archangel, and with the trump of God: and the dead in Christ shall rise first: Then we which are alive and remain shall be caught up together with them in the clouds, to meet the Lord in the air: and so shall we ever be with the Lord (I Thessalonians 4:16-18).

It is soon to take place! It is essential that we are ready for this great day.

> Wherefore seeing we also are compassed about with so great a cloud of witnesses, let us lay aside every weight, and the sin which doth so easily beset us, and let us run with patience the race that is set before us (Hebrews 12:1).

Weights are things which lay heavily upon our mind and spirit. They are things which keep us from giving our best to the Lord Jesus Christ, and sin is anything that separates us from Him.

This is not the time to become entangled with the things of this world. Jesus talked about entanglement in Luke 21:34-36. He said,

> And take heed to yourselves, lest at any time your hearts be overcharged with surfeiting, and drunkenness, and cares of this life, and so that day come upon you unawares. For as a snare shall it come on all them that dwell on the face of the whole earth. Watch ye therefore, and pray always, that ye may be accounted worthy to escape all these things that shall come to pass, and to stand before the Son of Man.

God never has, and never will, accept second best or anything less than our best. He will be the judge of what is each person's best. He established this truth when one of the scribes asked Jesus which was the first commandment of all.

> And Jesus answered him, The first of all the commandments is, Hear, O Israel; The Lord our God is one Lord: And thou shalt love the Lord thy God with all thy heart, and with all thy soul, and with all thy mind, and with all thy strength: this is the first commandment (Mark 12:29-30).

This is it! The Lord will not share His glory, nor will he sit on the same throne with another god, nor will He accept second best from His children, as the following Scriptures prove:

> I am the Lord: that is my name: and my glory will I not give to another, neither my praise to graven images (Isaiah 42:8).

> And the Philistines took the ark of God, and brought it from Eben-ezer unto Ashdod. When the Philistines took the ark of God, they brought it into the house of Dagon, and set it by Dagon. And when they of Ashdod arose early on the morrow, behold, Dagon was fallen upon his face to the earth before the ark of the Lord. And they took Dagon, and set him in his place again. And when they arose early on the morrow morning, behold, Dagon was fallen upon his face to the ground before the ark of the Lord; and the head of Dagon and both the palms of his hands were cut off upon the threshold; only the stump of Dagon was left to him. But the hand of the Lord was heavy upon them of Ashdod, and he destroyed them (I Samuel 5:1-4,6).

God would not allow the ark of God, which represented His presence, to sit side-by-side with a false god. He caused Dagon to fall on his face twice. There is not enough room in any heart for both God and other gods. He alone wants to be exalted. God commanded the people to worship only Him, as the following Scriptures demonstrate:

> Thou shalt not bow down thyself to them (other gods), nor serve them; for I the Lord thy God am a jealous God (Exodus 20:5).

> For thou shalt worship no other god: for the Lord, whose name is Jealous, is a jealous God (Exodus 34:14).

The well-known story of Cain and Abel needs to be mentioned here. Both Cain and Abel brought a sacrificial offering to the Lord, but only Abel's was accepted. "But unto Cain and to his offering he had not respect. And Cain was very wroth, and his countenance fell" (Genesis 4:5). God did not accept Cain's offering. Hebrews 11:4 reminds us that, "Abel offered unto God a more excellent sacrifice than Cain."

God will not tolerate shoddiness or less than the best from His people. Even though this is true, remember in your quest for excellence that you never can get good enough to be worthy of God. It is not your goodness God wants, it is your heart and your obedience to Him. He knows how much of your heart you give to Him by the choices you make and by the attitudes you have towards His commands. Acceptance by God is determined by your amount of surrender. He is not a halfway God and He will not accept a halfway attitude from His people either.

The concept of God accepting only the best is substantiated in Malachi 1.

> Ye offer polluted bread upon mine altar; and ye say, Wherein have we polluted thee? In that ye say, The table of the Lord is contemptible. And if ye offer the blind for sacrifice, is it not evil? and if ye offer the lame and sick, is it not evil? offer it now unto thy governor; will he be pleased with thee, or accept thy person? saith the Lord of hosts...Ye said also, Behold, what a weariness is it! and ye have snuffed at it, saith the Lord of hosts; and ye brought that which was torn,

> and the lame, and the sick; thus ye brought an offering: should I accept this of your hand? saith the Lord. But cursed be the deceiver, which hath in his flock a male, and voweth, and sacrificeth unto the Lord a corrupt thing: for I am a great King, saith the Lord of hosts (Malachi 1:7-8,13-14).

Corrupt means "that which is changed from a state of uprightness, correctness, truth, etc., to a bad state." It is "to change from good to bad; to debase or to falsify."

The Lord asked them if they would offer less than their best to a governor. God, who required the best of the flock for a sacrifice in Old Testament days, has not changed His standard. He still requires the best: the best being 100% of your heart.

There are some who advocate a doctrine of lesser consecration. They imply that it does not matter what you do, for somehow God will overlook it. However, God will not overlook anything that goes against His Word. He will forgive, He is merciful, but He is not sloppy or a push-over. This is proven over and over in the Scripture.

When King Uzziah's heart was lifted up, he entered into the office of the priest to offer incense, and the other priests told him that he was doing wrong. He became angry with them and leprosy appeared in his forehead. They then thrust him out of the temple. II Chronicles 26:20 says, "...the Lord had smitten him." To be smitten or cast away by God is a horrible thing.

Even more horrible is to be hated by God. Romans 9:13 records some spine-chilling words. "As it is written,

Jacob have I loved, but Esau have I hated." Where was this written? Malachi recorded it.

> The burden of the word of the Lord to Israel by Malachi. I have loved you, saith the Lord. Yet ye say, Wherein hast thou loved us? Was not Esau Jacob's brother? saith the Lord: yet I loved Jacob. And I hated Esau, and laid his mountains and his heritage waste for the dragons of the wilderness" (Malachi 1:1-3).

What did Esau do that was so terrible as to cause God's hatred toward him? Hebrews 12:16-17 gives a clue. "Lest there be any fornicator, or profane person, as Esau, who for one morsel of meat sold his birthright." God was astonished that any man would sell such a great blessing for one small meal, that at best provided nourishment for a twelve-hour time period.

He exchanged a whole life for one tiny meal. It is unthinkable, totally devoid of wisdom, unbelievable and downright foolish. He threw away gold for a piece of flesh. The Scripture describes Esau as a fornicator and profane. Full of idolatry and spiritual poverty, Esau violated his birthright by irreverence. He desecrated and showed contempt for that which was sacred. He defiled that which was holy and God-given.

Not only did Esau toss away his birthright in a moment of physical weakness, but he lived to regret it. He sought to change his father's mind. Esau repented, shed tears and pled with his father, but Isaac rejected him. Hebrews 12:17 says, "For ye know how that afterward, when he would have inherited the blessing, he was rejected: for he found no place of repentance, though he sought it carefully with tears."

After reading this portion of Scripture, you should not feel that God will not forgive you. He said He would in no wise cast out anyone who comes to Him in repentance. The story of Esau is inserted here to both warn and challenge you at the same time. Be careful how you treat what God has given you. For example, if God gives you talent in some area, and you never develop it for His glory, you are in a sense like Esau. You may be God's child, just as Esau was still Isaac's child, but you are ignoring and disregarding that which could bring a blessing to you and to many others.

Psalm 65:4 brings to our attention the concept that God can choose to accept or not accept our offering or service. It says,

> Blessed is the man whom thou choosest, and causeth to approach unto thee, that he may dwell in thy courts: we shall be satisfied with the goodness of thy house, even of thy holy temple.

This concept is supported by the parable of the talents in Matthew 25. Jesus told a story about three men who were each given talents by their lord, who then went on a journey. The first one was given five talents; the second one, two talents; and the third one, one talent. When the lord returned, he called each of them to him and asked an account of what they did with the talents he had given them.

The first man said that he had increased his five talents to ten. The second man increased his from two to four. These two men received a blessing of acceptance and approval from their lord. Verse 21 says, "Well done, thou good and faithful servant; thou hast been faithful over a few things, I will make thee ruler over many things: enter thou into the joy of thy lord."

The third man gave a different report. He said, "Lord, I knew thee that thou art an hard man, reaping where thou hast not sown...And I was afraid, and went and hid thy talent in the earth: lo, there thou hast that is thine" (verses 24-25).

What was the lord's response?

> Thou wicked and slothful servant, thou knewest that I reap where I sowed not...Take therefore the talent from him, and give it unto him which hath ten talents...And cast ye the unprofitable servant into outer darkness: there shall be weeping and gnashing of teeth (verses 26-30).

What was Christ trying to tell us? He wants us to reverence that which He has given us and not waste it away by slothful, undisciplined living. His gifts are sacred to Him, and we must treat them as such. He does not want anyone comparing himself with anyone else; He just wants each person to be a good steward over that which

He has entrusted into his hand. The Lord knows who is throwing away or burying a God-given talent.

An unknown author wrote,

> God does not give to everyone the same abilities...Some gained the advantage in heritage, in training or through opportunities...God will reward the person who did the *best* with his given talents. He will bless the one who accepted responsibility and was loyal to it. But, in none of his teachings do we find leniency for those not found faithful. [2]

He knows whether you are giving your best or settling for less. It all boils down to one question: Who or what is your master? What is important to you? To whom or to what do you devote most of your time? What dominates your life, excellence or disorder?

All Christians will have to decide to what they will be faithful, and whom or what they will serve, for Jesus said, "No man can serve two masters: for either he will hate the one, and love the other; or else he will hold to the one, and despise the other. Ye cannot serve God and mammon" (Matthew 6:24).

This is the day to shatter and demolish our idols. John MacNeil wrote,

> If we shatter them, there will rain about our hearts the very treasures of heaven, the gifts and graces of the Holy Spirit. If you do not crown Him Lord of all, you do not crown Him Lord at all. [3]

As the ocean, wind and universe give obeisance to their Creator, so must mankind turn away from self-absorption to God. A.J. Morris wrote,

> It is the end and essence of all religion to turn the mind from self to God; to give it absorbing views of the Divine beauty and glory; to fill it with Divine love and zeal; to make it feel that nothing is good enough or great enough for Him. [4]

This is the hour to hunger and thirst after Him, for the sighs of a heart deeply hungering are to God sweet incense. Jesus said in Matthew 5:6, "Blessed are they which do hunger and thirst after righteousness: for they shall be filled."

As we approach God, and as we hunger and thirst after righteousness, we must realize that we have been made kings and priests unto God (Revelation 1:6). It is important that we keep ourselves clean before Him.

> No priest was to officiate at the altar in a state of unfitness, under penalty of excommunication. "That soul shall be cut off from my presence: I am the Lord." This declares the priest to be fallible and frail; need for constant watchfulness lest the altar become polluted. Under the new dispensation a fountain full and free is open for sin and uncleanness. As kings and priests unto God, believers are expected to exhibit in their lives the fruits of the Spirit. Christianity has not relaxed the demands of the law for holiness of the character, the

standard is even higher, for "If any man have not the spirit of Christ, he is none of his."

The sacrifice, not the officiating priest, was the centre of the Levitical economy. He existed for the altar, not it for him. Every offering was to be presented without blemish. No unwholesome or unsightly thing was to be laid on the altar. The Highest deserved, as He demanded, the best. God still demands the best we can offer. [5]

Are you going to choose to give your best to the Master or will you be as the individual described in the poem below?

Who is Worse?
One who does not believe in God, or
One who believes in Him, but does not serve Him?
One who does not believe the Bible, or
One who believes in the Bible but does not read it?
One who does not believe in prayer, or
One who believes in prayer, but never prays?
One who does not believe in church, or
One who believes in church, but never attends,
Does not support it regularly, does not pray for it
And very often criticizes it?

Author unknown [6]

Giving God our best is wrapped up in many little things. It is not one big moment, but it consists of trifles.

Michelangelo said, “Trifles make perfection, but perfection is no trifle.” The little things do matter. Whether or not we are giving our best to God is determined not only by our approach to Him, but by our approach to one another. The things we may consider unimportant are often the most important of all. The way we treat a child, how we approach the clerk in a store, or the manner in which we conduct ourselves with our family is considered by God to be the next thing on the agenda, after Him. He is first, our neighbor is second. It is impossible to give God our best when we treat others shabbily.

Before we can please God, we must come to grips with the fact that we are immortal beings. We must know who we are and remember that we are part of a great plan. Life on earth is not just a few years that are quickly over, but life is forever. We should treat it as such. George H. Hepworth said it like this:

> I am immortal! I should never forget it, but should carry myself as one who cherishes that truth. No matter what my condition in life may be, whether I be poor or rich, learned or unlettered, well or ill, struggling or at leisure, I am immortal. I shall outlive my body and my sorrows, my tears and my sighs, all hardships and heartbreakings, for God—my God—will help me through it all. [7]

We are immortal souls that will live forever. This world we live in is just a dressing room for eternity. While we are going about our business it is imperative that we stand in awe of God and seek to please Him. Psalm 33:8 says, “Let all the earth fear the Lord: let all the inhabitants of the world stand in awe of him.”

He is to be feared and reverenced. Psalm 89:7 says, “God is greatly to be feared in the assembly of the saints, and to be had in reverence of all them that are about you.”

"For what are men better than sheep or goats
That nourish a blind life within the brain,
If, knowing God, they lift not hands of prayer
Both for themselves and those who call them friend.
More things are wrought by prayer
Than this world dreams of."

Tennyson

CHAPTER 2

GIVE YOUR BEST TO PRAYER

Dr. A.J. Gordon wrote about the prayer life of David Brainerd.

In the depths of those forests, alone, unable to speak the language of the Indians, he spent whole days literally in prayer. What was he praying for? He knew that he could not reach the people; he did not understand their language. If he wanted to speak at all, he must find somebody who could vaguely interpret his thought; therefore he knew that anything he should do must be absolutely dependent upon the power of God.

So he spent whole days in prayer, simply that the power of the Holy Ghost might come upon him so unmistakably that these people should not be able to

> stand before him. What was his answer? Once he preached and the interpreter was so intoxicated that he could hardly stand up. That was the best he could do. Yet scores were converted through that sermon. We can account for it only by the tremendous power of God behind him. [1]

Brainerd exemplified what the writer wrote in the following psalm: "My soul longeth, yea, even fainteth for the courts of the Lord: my heart and my flesh crieth out for the living God" (Psalm 84:2).

Prayer is the most powerful form of energy available to man. When we pray we connect ourselves with the incomparable God of the universe. Prayer gives us strength, inspiration, direction, stamina, moral purity, and joy. When humanity touches Divinity, something grand happens.

The only way life can be lived successfully is through keeping in direct communication with the Master. Whenever we get out of touch with the Master, we are dead spiritually. Those who have no prayer life have no spiritual life and are not in touch with great things. Their lives are powerless and meaningless in the light of eternity.

The great strategy of the tempter is to get God's people to neglect prayer. His program is the mad rush of dates, excitement, fleshly display and indulgence, so there will be no time to think life through properly and to sit trembling with awe in the presence of the Lord.

Prayer is the bridge to span the chasm between the real self and the self which one seeks to become. In moments of intense prayer the fervent soul lays before God the longings about which he feels strongly, and the Lord answers with love. Prayer knows no defeat. It is the best way to become that person you were created to be.

It is imperative that you keep a check on yourself. Jesus said the way to take heed to oneself, and to be ready for His coming, was to pray always. Luke 21:36 says, "Watch ye therefore, and pray always, that ye may be accounted worthy to escape all these things that shall come to pass, and to stand before the Son of man."

The Lord spoke to me several years ago about the need for people to pray in a united way. Then in September 1994, He impressed me with the fact that He wanted His people to establish prayer capitals and a network of prayer that would encircle the globe. I shared it with my husband and wrote it down, praying that it would come to pass. Prayer is the key to power and is man's link with God. James 4:8 says, "Draw nigh to God, and he will draw nigh to you." What an awesome thing, for finite man to have the infinite, Almighty God draw nigh to him when he would make an overture toward Him. Prayer is communication between earth and heaven. There are no barriers in prayer. The influence of prayer has been felt around the world, and many are the stories that document this. One of my favorite has to do with the *Titanic.*

One Sunday night in April 1912, an American woman could not sleep because of an oppression of fear. At last she felt a burden of prayer, and with tremendous earnestness began to pray for her husband who was then in the mid-Atlantic, homeward bound on the *Titanic*. As the hours went by she could get no assurance, and kept on praying in an agony, until about five o'clock in the morning when a great peace came to her, and she slept.

Meanwhile her husband, Colonel Gracie, was among the doomed hundreds who were trying frantically to launch the lifeboats from the great ship whose vitals had been torn out by an iceberg. He had given up all hope of being saved himself, and was doing his best to help the women and children. He wished that he could get a last message through to his wife, and cried from his heart, "Good-by, my darling." Then as the ship plunged to her watery grave, he was sucked down in the giant whirlpool.

Suddenly he came to the surface and found himself near an overturned life boat. Along with several others he climbed aboard, and was picked up by another lifeboat, at about five in the morning, the very time that peace came to his praying wife. Her prayer was not hemmed in by the four walls of the room in which she was praying, but it reached out into a roaring ocean. This kind of prayer is a prayer of supplication. It will not take no for an answer, but will storm the battlements of heaven and bring confusion and defeat to all the powers of hell.

James 5:16-18 says,

> Confess your faults one to another, and pray one for another, that ye may be healed. The effectual fervent prayer of a righteous man availeth much. Elias was a man subject to like passions as we are, and he prayed earnestly that it might not rain: and it rained not on the earth by the space of three years and six months. And

he prayed again, and the heaven gave rain, and the earth brought forth her fruit.

Elijah was subject to passions as we are, yet he prayed. Everyone must decide which passion they will be subject to: the passion of prayer, the passion of lustful desires or the passion of pleasure. Everyone chooses their destiny by their choices. Elijah chose to pray.

James Hastings wrote this about Elijah:

> He comes down from the hills of Gilead as the champion and prophet of Jehovah in the dark days of Israel's apostasy. He comes to bear witness to truths which ought never to have been denied in Israel. Like every true reformer, he takes his stand upon Old Principles. He is the personified conscience of the nation. He comes, a prophet of heroic mold, to witness by deeds rather than words. [2]

Elijah was just like everyone else in the fact that he had the same passions and desires. It was his lifestyle, his separation from the normal, his life of prayer, fasting, humility and faith that made him bold in God. What were his controlling passions?

1. *He loved Jehovah God.* His ruling passion was jealousy for the Lord God of hosts (I Kings 19:10).

2. *He hated sin and indecision towards God.* His spirit blazed with fire over the indecision and idolatry of the people (I Kings 18:17-21).

3. *He was a humble man.* He wrapped his face in his mantle, a mark of humility (I Kings 19:13). He also put his face between his knees (I Kings 18:42).

4. *He separated himself unto the Lord.* He fasted for forty days (I Kings 19:8).

Consistent fervent prayer opens the doors to miracles. This was true in the life of Bill Drost, a missionary to South America. The following story is related in his biography, *Man With a Destiny.* (Portions of this story are quoted directly from that work.)

Before going as a missionary, he first served as a soldier in the Canadian Army. One Saturday when all the men had a day off to spend as they liked, everybody went to town except Bill. Knowing the shooting range would be deserted, he went there to pray.

While Bill was praying, the Lord told him to go to the Pembroke hospital. Under compulsion from the Holy Spirit, he went back to the barracks to change into his dress uniform. Just as he stepped out of the door, an officer driving up in a Jeep stopped and asked if he was going out. "Yes sir, I am," answered Bill.

The officer said, "Jump in, then." Bill jumped in and off they went until they reached the outside gate. Bill tapped the captain on the arm and said, "Excuse me, sir, but since I was not planning to go out I didn't collect a pass."

"Don't worry, you're with an officer. Just sit still and be calm," said the captain.

So it was, young Bill was escorted right to the place the Lord had told him to go. When he arrived inside the hospital, he did not know where to go and wandered around until he noticed a door which had a "No Visitors Allowed" sign on it. This seemed to be the place to which he was drawn, and he made his way towards it.

The door was opened a fraction, and somebody inside was sobbing heavily. He pushed the door open an inch or two and peered in. On the bed, lying very still, was a small body bandaged from head to toe, with only a patch of forehead visible and slits for the eyes. Judging from the size, Bill thought it must be a boy around fourteen. His eyes went down the bed to the sound of the sobbing. Kneeling at the foot was a lady, obviously the boy's mother, who cried convulsively as she made her desperate prayers. The bedclothes at the bottom were knotted from her small white fists working out her agony on them. He was moved with compassion for her, and pushing open the door, tiptoed over.

"Lady, my dear woman, can I help you?" he said tenderly, touching her on the shoulder.

She looked up at Bill, startled, then asked, "Oh, are you Pentecostal? I have been praying the Lord would send someone to pray for my boy. He has been in a terrible accident. There is no hope for him. Will you pray for him?"

she pleaded, her faith striving, grasping and hoping in the presence of this unexpected visitor.

"Yes, I will pray." Bill went immediately to the head of the bed. Putting his hands on the boy's head he commanded, "Jesus, heal this boy *now*."

At that moment the boy opened his eyes and looked at his mother. "Mum, why are you crying?" he asked.

"Oh, son! You can speak to me!" the mother exclaimed.

"Yes, I'm alright now...Jesus has put his hands on my head. I know I'm alright now."

Unprepared for the emotional scene that followed, Bill quickly left the hospital. Three days later, Bill went back to the hospital to see how the boy was doing. When he stepped through the door, a nurse from the desk went running over to him. She asked excitedly, "Are you the soldier who came to see the little boy who was run over with a steel roller?"

He acknowledged that he was and inquired if he could see the boy. She told him that the boy had been sent to Ottawa for tests and that nobody could believe the instant miraculous healing that had taken place. She went and got the doctors who had wanted to see him if he came back to the hospital. Soon doctors and nurses were buzzing around him, asking questions. They were all very impressed by what had occurred, and when the facts came out it was little wonder. The boy had been run over by a steel roller which crushed practically everything inside him. The doctors in Ottawa found the boy to be completely whole and released him. [3]

What if Bill Drost had not gone to the shooting range to pray that day? What if he had not followed the voice of the Lord and gone to the Pembroke hospital? What if he had not been sensitive to the voice of the Holy Ghost? How many people are waiting for us to be people of prayer and for us to be sensitive to the voice of the Spirit?

Mrs. Charles Cowman wrote,

> Would you like to be a radiant Christian? Spend time in prayer. You cannot be a radiant Christian any other way. You cannot have vital faith in God if you give all your time to the world and to secular affairs, to reading the newspapers and to reading literature, no matter how good it is. [4]

Make time to give your best to prayer.

> [Prayer] is the whole personality–intellect as well as emotion and will–energizing in fellowship with the Lord of all life. It is man consciously apprehending his high destiny and stretching towards it. It is not merely one of the noblest and most fruitful activities of the soul, at once the most intensely individual and the most comprehensively social, but the fount and the consummation of all noble activity. [5]

Prayer is more than just a petition. Steven Mosley shares in the book, *A Tale of Three Virtues,* some thoughts about prayer.

Normally we equate prayer with a single aspect of it: petition. Prayer is asking for things—a hurried request for watchcare before we rush out the door. But a quick nod heavenward, like thumbing the Bible for a quick fix, does not create a devotional life. If we want to become artists and not just day laborers, prayer must become more devotion than transaction. Petition is vitally important, but praise is what best helps develop the essential discipline of seeing. It's a way of looking intently at God.

Our natural tendency in prayer is to touch every base except God Himself. We tug at His blessings; intercede for others; express thanks for the trees, our job, new furniture, sunny days. We do everything but focus on...God. [6]

One of the main goals of prayer should be to learn how to focus on the power and presence of God, and to help others to do this also. The *ultimate* purpose of prayer is to achieve not things, but spiritual victory, *and* to see things the way God sees them. We are instructed to "Let this mind be in you, which was also in Christ Jesus" (Philippians 2:5). Prayer helps this to transpire.

"Christ has no hands but our hands to do His work today
He has no feet but our feet to lead men in the way
He has no tongue but our tongue to tell them how He died
He has no help but our help to bring them to His side."

Annie Johnston Flint

CHAPTER 3

GIVE YOUR BEST TO COMPASSION AND EVANGELISM

The following poem describes what we should be:

We are not storehouses, but channels,
We are not cisterns, but springs,
Passing our benefits onward,
Fitting our blessings with wings;
Letting the water flow onward
To spread o'er the desert forlorn:
Sharing our bread with our brothers,
Our comfort with those who mourn. [1]

Did not Jesus say that out of our bellies would flow rivers of living water? How many people have been healed by your flowing river? How many have felt your compassion this week? How many lives have been changed simply because you took the time to make a difference? Are you too busy to feed the multitude or help the lone woman by the well? Of what does your life consist? Is it filled with compassion or is it filled with the busyness of self-gratification?

Do you have the qualities of the good Samaritan, or are you as the priest and Levite, looking the part on the outside, but dead inside to the feelings of those who are hurting? What are you doing with the oil the Lord has given to you? Are you storing and saving it for that grand day when you will do that great thing the Lord has called you to do, or are you daily ministering a little oil to this one and a little oil to that one on the road of life, helping whoever you can, even though nobody may know about it?

Louise Barker Barnhill wrote,

> With trembling hand the lonely beggar knocks. Cautiously the door cracks narrowly ajar and fear peers out on ragged want. At once the door slams shut, and as the beggar turns to go, the winds of cold indifference buffet him anew. For one brief pause he looks upon the passing throng, then quietly he moves to lose himself therein. Where does he go? Beggars? The world is filled with those who starve—hungering, ever hungering for love. Hear them as they cry: "Love me with

> your heart, not with your shallow self alone. Love me for what I am—my frailties—my differences—not by the measure of society. Love me for the sake of love—enough to help me." Time is autumn old, and ere its chill becomes the frost and snow of winter's dress, compassion fires must burn with brighter glow. Jesus said: "Inasmuch as ye did it unto the least of these, my brethren, ye have done it unto me" (Matthew 25:40). Even now a beggar knocks. [2]

Reproducing the life of Jesus and reflecting His light is life's biggest business. When Jesus cast unclean spirits out of the maniac of Gadara, He sent him home to his friends and told him to tell them two things. What were the two things Jesus wanted emphasized? Mark 5:19 says, "Howbeit Jesus suffered him not, but saith unto him, Go home to thy friends, and tell them how great things the Lord hath done for thee, and hath had *compassion* on thee."

Jesus emphasized compassion, and so should we. Compassion is more than sympathy. Compassion moves beyond feeling sympathetic; it shows responsive action. It shows tender mercy, kindness and heartfelt love. This is the day to reach out as never before, for the world is groping in darkness for an answer, and are interested in the supernatural. We as Christians have the answer. Age, cultural background, or training does not matter; what matters is the fact that we have the *Bread of life* and people are hungry.

In the mountains of Columbia, South America, is a village called La Morena. There is a group of people there that knows about Jesus simply because of a 17-year-old girl named Eucaris. (Portions of the following story are quoted directly from *Man with a Destiny.*)

When Bill and Ruth Drost took the gospel to Cali, Columbia, one of their first converts was Eucaris. She was radiantly joyful, but also became burdened for her relatives in La Morena, so she asked Missionary Drost if she could go up and tell her people about this glorious gospel. When he saw her resolve in the Spirit, and her undaunted and powerful determination to do something for Jesus Christ, he said, "Go, in Jesus' Name!"

After packing her few belongings, she plodded up the mountain, through the banana and coffee plantations, praying persistently that God would help her speak to the people. Many recognized and greeted her, and she used this opportunity to mention her experience and to invite them to a meeting she planned to hold at her parent's home.

Meanwhile, Saul, the cousin of Eucaris, was feeling edgy, like something unusual was going on, but he did not know what it was. He owned the only saloon in that mountain area, known as The Last Chance Saloon. When 7:00 p.m. arrived and not one man had appeared, he knew something was wrong. About that time he heard the sound of hooves outside, and running outside he hollered, "Hey, what's going on? Where is everybody tonight?"

The man on the horse replied, "Oh, haven't you heard? Everybody's at the gospel meeting that girl is holding.

Young Eucaris, your cousin, found religion while she was in Cali. Anyway, everybody is there to listen to her. I'm just on my way." And off he rode in the night.

Saul was wild. Eucaris, his smart bit of a cousin, playing the big shot because she'd been to Cali! Who did she think she was anyway? He'd soon fix her. Saul ran back into the bar and put on double holsters, quickly made ready his horse and tore down the mountain track furiously, determined to settle this nonsense. Religion—he'd soon show them!

Approaching the house he saw many animals tied outside in the moonlight. Instantly he dismounted, tethering his horse to a branch with a quick flick. Glancing through the window, he took in the situation. Sure enough, his cousin was there—she seemed to be praying or something—with people who were kneeling down. Now was the time. Pulling himself to his full height and throwing his chest out, he barged through the door with his shoulder in a dramatic entrance, hands on pistols.

But that was as far as he got.

Eucaris had never felt such a spirit of evangelism. She recited all she had seen happen in Cali, and preached a down-to-earth message on the love of God and the need to repent. Telling simple stories, the folks had come under tremendous conviction, and some were weeping, many getting right with God. Eucaris wept with them, praying earnestly for God to baptize them with His Spirit.

At that moment, cousin Saul came in with a bang. Looking up startled, Eucaris took in the situation and prayed that God would stop Saul from ruining the meeting.

Saul couldn't move. He stood transfixed at the door, dazed and confused. It was like in a dream; nothing would move, not an arm, not a finger, not an eyelid. He could have been enclosed in warm, transparent steel. People in the room continued kneeling in prayer. Suddenly, in the atmosphere, he felt tremendously unclean; his cousin came towards him in seeming slow motion; she looked radiantly beautiful and she looked...*clean.* The dark eyes of Eucaris looked at him from unplumbed depths, with a tenderness he had never seen. It was as though some other force was in those eyes. Saul wilted as he looked into them. She put her hands on his head and he felt fire go through him as she said, "You need Jesus."

At that moment, released from the force that held him, he dropped to his knees. He could do no more. All he wanted to do was cry and confess and be free from the horror of his condition, to find the beauty he perceived about him. Saul stayed there a long time. When he did get up, the first thing he did was to go back to his bar and pour all his liquor down the mountainside. He was through with it, forever." [3]

There are many more Sauls, friends and relatives waiting for a Eucaris to come and tell them about Jesus and a better life. All it takes is being filled with the Spirit of God, a heart on fire with love, and taking the first step. The following essay throbs with the passion of care.

What is Evangelism?

It is the sob of God.

It is the anguished cry of Jesus as He weeps over a doomed city.

It is the cry of Paul, "I could wish that myself were accursed from Christ for my brethren, my kinsmen according to the flesh."

It is the sob of parents in the night, weeping over a prodigal child.

It is the secret of a great church.

It is the secret of a great preacher and of a great Christian.

Author unknown [4]

There are only two people that keep you from being involved in evangelism: Satan and yourself. You have been promised power over Satan, for I John 4:4 says, "...Greater is he that is in you, than he that is in the world." Satan would like you to believe fallacies and untruths, anything to keep you from bringing the gospel of Jesus Christ to the world.

The following saying from an imaginary certificate is a believer's active permit to not help evangelize:

The bearer of this certificate is disqualified from the service of introducing others to Jesus Christ inasmuch as:

He already has enough religious duties.

He doesn't feel called as a soul-winner.

He has fears which hinder such a work.

He feels it is really the pastor's job.
CERTIFIED: Satan [5]

The problem lies within ourselves. We must be dead to pride and laziness and thrust ourselves forward, working together as a mighty army in every burg, tribe, community, city, country, nation and continent. This is the day to just do it!

The story is told of John Sung who came to America in 1920 to work on his doctorate in chemistry. While in America, the call of Christ came to him. Soon afterwards, he had a most unusual dream in which he saw himself in a casket. God seemed to say to him, "John Sung is dead: dead to self, but alive to Christ!"

Then it seemed that the corpse began to stir. Angels began to weep. "Don't weep, angels," said John. "I will remain dead to the world and live only for the Christ."

This should be the cry of every Christian: "I am dead to the world and will live only for Christ, helping others find their way to a better life and fulfillment in Him."

"The Bible is a window in this prison of hope, through which we look into eternity."

John Sullivan Dwight

CHAPTER 4

GIVE YOUR BEST TO THE STUDY OF THE WORD

When Sir Walter Scott lay dying, he cried, "Bring me the Book." His nephew said, "Which book, sir?" And Scott replied, "Young man, there is but one book, the Bible." [1]

The Swedish Nightingale, Jenny Lind, won great success as an operatic singer, and money poured into her purse. Yet she left the stage when singing her best and never went back to it. Once an English friend found her sitting by the sea, looking out into the glory of a sunset. They talked and the conversation led to the question of why she abandoned the stage at the height of her success.

"When, every day," was the quiet answer, "it made me think less of the Bible and nothing at all of that (pointing to the sunset). What else could I do?"

There is nothing else on earth more important than the precious Word of God. It should be revered, studied, memorized and treated with respect. Years ago before the war in Poland, a humble villager received a Bible from a missionary who visited his small hamlet. He read it, was converted to Jesus, and passed the book on to others. Through that one Bible 200 more people became believers.

When the missionary revisited the town in the summer of 1940, the group gathered to worship and listen to his preaching. The missionary suggested that instead of giving the customary testimonies they all recite verses of Scripture.

Thereupon a man arose and asked, "Perhaps we have misunderstood. Did you mean verses or chapters?"

"Do you mean to say there are people here who can recite chapters of the Bible?" asked Mr. Billester in astonishment.

Those villagers had memorized not only chapters, but whole books of the Bible. Thirteen knew Matthew and Luke and half of Genesis. One had committed all the Psalms to memory. Together, the two hundred knew virtually the entire Bible. Passed around from family to family and brought to the gathering on Sundays, the old Book had become so worn with use that its pages were hardly legible.

On the other hand, it is possible to have a worn-out Bible but not know anything about it. A church member remarked to a minister that the Bible on the table was about worn out. It did indeed appear so, but a closer examination revealed that it was only worn on the outside; the inside was intact. The Bible had been abused rather than used.

The Mohammedans' sacred book is known as the Koran, a book smaller than our New Testament. It is written in Arabic, which is considered a sacred language. The Mohammedans never touch the book with unwashed hands, never carry it below the waistline, and never place it upon the floor, although it is customary to place everything else upon the floor in Mohammedan lands.

It is time to place the Word at the top of the list of all reading material. It needs to be highly exalted. Psalm 138:2 says, "I will worship toward thy holy temple, and praise thy name for thy loving kindness and for thy truth: for thou hast magnified thy word above all thy name." If God has magnified it, we sin if we do not magnify it also.

Hebrews 4:12 sparkles with truth. It says,

> For the word of God is quick, and powerful, and sharper than any twoedged sword, piercing even to the dividing asunder of soul and spirit, and of the joints and marrow, and is a discerner of the thoughts and intents of the heart.

Do you know of anything else more powerful?

Not only does it discern the thoughts, but the Word enters the chambers of men's and women's hearts and mingles in all the sorrows and joys of life. It ministers comfort in the hours of trouble and it lights the fire of a dream that was almost dead. People rest in the Bible. It is a book of hope, light, and direction. It should be studied and pored over until it becomes familiar to you.

It can be trusted. Dr. Robert Dick Wilson, former professor of Semitic philology at Princeton Theological Seminary, said,

> After forty-five years of scholarly research in biblical textual studies and in language study, I have come now to the conviction that no man knows enough to assail the truthfulness of the Old Testament. Where there is sufficient documentary evidence to make an investigation, the statements of the Bible, in the original text, have stood the test. [2]

Dr. J.O. Kinnaman said,

> Of the hundreds of thousands of artifacts found by the archaeologists, not one has ever been discovered that contradicts or denies one word, phrase, clause, or sentence of the Bible, but always confirms and verifies the facts of the Biblical record. [3]

Over 100 years ago, William Ramsay, a young English scholar, went to Asia Minor with the expressed purpose of proving that the history given by Luke in his gospel and in the Acts was inaccurate. His professors had confidently said that Luke could not be right.

He began to dig in the ancient ruins of Greece and Asia Minor, testing for ancient terms, boundaries, and other items which would indicate if a writer had been inventing this history at a later date as his professors had claimed. To his amazement, he found that the New Testament Scriptures were accurate to the tiniest detail. So convincing was the evidence that Ramsay himself became a great Biblical scholar. Many look upon Sir William Ramsay's book as being a classic concerning the history of the New Testament.

You can study the Bible without any hesitation to its authenticity. It has been proven to be true over and over again. Walter F. Burke, general manager of Projects Mercury and Gemini, and who at one time was vice-president of the McDonnell Aircraft Corporation, declared in an interview,

> I have found nothing in science or space exploration to compel me to throw away my Bible or to reject my Saviour, Jesus Christ, in whom I trust. The space age has been a factor in the deepening of my own spiritual life. I read the Bible more now. I get from the Bible what I cannot get from science: the really important things of life. [4]

Great men of renown felt that study of the Bible was very important. The following statements represent their sentiments:

George Washington:
"It is impossible to rightly govern the world without God and the Bible."

John Quincy Adams:
"So great is my veneration of the Bible, that the earlier my children begin to read it the more confident will be my hope that they will prove useful citizens of their country and respectable members of society."

Charles Dickens:
"The New Testament is the very best book that ever was or ever will be known in the world."

Andrew Jackson:
"That book, sir, is the rock on which our republic rests."

Abraham Lincoln:
"I believe the Bible is the best gift God has ever given to man. All the good from the Saviour of the world is communicated to us through this book."

Horace Greeley:
"It is impossible to mentally or socially enslave a Bible-reading people. The principles of the Bible are the groundwork of human freedom."

Woodrow Wilson:
"I ask every man and woman in this audience that from

this day on they will realize that part of the destiny of America lies in their daily perusal of this great book."

Douglas MacArthur:
"Believe me, sir, never a night goes by, be I ever so tired, but I read the Word of God before I go to bed."

Herbert Hoover:
"The whole of the inspiration of our civilization springs from the teachings of Christ and the lessons of the Prophets. To read the Bible for these fundamentals is a necessity of American life."

Dwight D. Eisenhower:
"To read the Bible is to take a trip to a fair land where the spirit is strengthened and faith renewed."

John Harvard, first president of Harvard University:
"Let every student be plainly instructed and earnestly pressed to consider well the main ends of his life and studies; to know God and...to lay Christ in the bottom as the only foundation of all knowledge and learning and see that the Lord only giveth wisdom. Let everyone seriously set himself by prayer in secret to see Christ as Lord and Master." [5]

Five years after establishing the Massachusetts Bay Colony, the Puritans started, in Boston, the first elementary school supported by tax money. In 1647, they passed an ordinance which marked the beginning of the U.S. public school system.

Among other things, the ordinance required at least one qualified teacher for every fifty householders, and a grammar school in every town of more than 100 families. It also put the Bible in the center of its curriculum, asserting that it is "one chief project of that old deluder, Satan, to keep men from the knowledge of the Scriptures." [6]

They had the right idea back in the 1600's, but it looks like many have come under the influence of that old "deluder," as our forefathers called him. It is time to do something about the poverty of the Scriptures in this generation.

You can help eradicate this problem, if you care enough to do so. Let us bring back the reverence for the Word of God and hunger after its teachings, upon which all the universe rests.

The Word of God is the most liberating book you can read. It is not bound by anyone or anything. It is a light in the darkness.

During the years of the martyrs, Christians fled into the underground caverns outside Rome in almost 600 miles of molelike tunnels. Ten generations of Christians were buried in the catacombs during approximately 300 years of suppression. No one knows the exact number, but archaeologists estimate between 1,750,000 and 4,000,000 Christians were interred in the dark tunnels.

What was their hope? Inscriptions of Scripture can still be seen on the catacomb walls. One of the most frequent inscriptions is the sign of the fish. However, the inscription which best describes their faith says, "The Word of God is not bound."

The power of the Word of God can transcend enemy lines, go into prison, and give hope in a dismal situation. On the wall of a cellar in Cologne, Germany, after World War II were found these words:

I BELIEVE

I Believe in the sun,
Even when it is not shining;
I Believe in love,
Even when I feel it not;
I believe in God,
Even when He is silent. [7]

The true story of the *Mutiny on the Bounty* has often been retold. One part that deserves retelling was the transformation wrought by one book. Nine mutineers with six Tahitian men and twelve Tahitian women put ashore on Pitcairn Island in 1790. One sailor soon began distilling alcohol, and the little colony was plunged into debauchery and vice.

Ten years later, only one white man survived, surrounded by the Tahitian women and their children. One day this sailor found a Bible in an old chest from the *Bounty*. He began to read it and then teach it to the others. The result was that his own life and ultimately the lives of all those in the colony were changed. Discovered in 1808 by the *USS Topas*, Pitcairn had become a prosperous community with no jail, no whiskey, no crime, and no laziness.

The truths of the Bible are like gold in the soil. Whole generations walk over the soil and do not know what treasures lie hidden beneath. People through the centuries do the same thing with the Bible.

J.W. Alexander penned the following words full of truth and power: "The study of God's word for the purpose of discovering God's will is the secret discipline which has formed the greatest characters." [8]

"Experience shows that success is due less to ability than zeal. The winner is he who gives himself to his work, body and soul."

Charles Buxton

"Without passion; religion, history, romance and art would be useless."

Honore De Balzac

CHAPTER 5

GIVE YOUR BEST TO PASSION AND ZEAL

Martin Luther told the following story about the devil's strategy.

The devil held a great anniversary, at which his emissaries were convened to report the results of their several missions. "I let loose the wild beasts of the desert," said one, "on a caravan of Christians; and their bones are now bleaching on the sands."

"What of that?" said the devil, "their souls were all saved."

"For ten years, I tried to get a single Christian asleep," said a third; "and I succeeded, and left him so."

Then the devil shouted, and the night stars of hell sang for joy. [1]

If the devil can get you to go to sleep, he will have your soul, for to sleep spiritually is to be dead. Paul in Ephesians 5:14 instructed the Christians to "Awake thou that sleepest, and rise from the dead."

Now is the time to be on fire and full of enthusiasm about the cause of God. The word *enthusiasm* comes from two Greek words, *en* and *theos,* meaning "God in us." At Pentecost, the Spirit of the Lord descended and filled all of them who were in the upper room. Christianity became dynamic after that waiting and infilling. Thousands of people were led to the Master by the driving power of this divine force. It was as fire shut up in their bones. It caused passionate living for a perfect Christ.

The very fiber of the early Church was filled with such fire that it swept the whole countryside. It was said to the apostles by the high priest, "Ye have filled Jerusalem with your doctrine" (Acts 5:28). They were persecuted, beaten and thrown into prison, but nothing could put out their fire. When they were released, where were they found? Acts 5:42 says, "And daily in the temple, and in every house, they ceased not to teach and preach Jesus Christ."

Each generation has had its reformers, or those with "hot" hearts. It is not the sophisticated and polished that change things, it is the passionate, zeal-filled individuals.

Alexander McLaren wrote, "It was not Erasmus, the polished, learned, scintillating intellect of his time, who made Germany over; it was rough, rugged Martin Luther with a conviction and compassion as deep as life." [2]

It is time for some more reformers, those whose hearts are stirred by the debauchery of a world gone mad. Pray the following prayer fervently and seek to become a flame in the night to light the way for those who are groping in darkness.

Give me the *love* that leads the way
The *faith* that nothing can dismay,
The *hope* no disappointments tire,
The *passion* that will burn like fire.
Let me not sink to become a clod:
Make me Thy fuel, Flame of God.

Author unknown [3]

What are you passionate about? What are you doing with your life? What stirs you to action? With what are you involved? The plans and purposes of people are an index to their character, especially when viewed in the light of the motives behind these purposes. The supreme objective of each person should be to do the will and purpose of God wholeheartedly.

The following words, penned 75 years ago by an unknown author, still have the passion with which they were written.

> Great souls love to deal in influences of permanent value. Eternity and God's program hold central place in the heart thought of great souls. They revel in world-wide plans for the betterment of the race. Nothing gladdens their hearts more than to know of tremendous undertakings to afford more people opportunities for life, liberty and the pursuit of happiness.
>
> They have a passion to help along every great and good cause. This passion of delight in service makes great souls radiant and interesting across the years....A great aim for a lifetime is vital. No aim is almost as disastrous as low aim. Great souls under the direct spiritual touch of God will have great purposes grow up in their lives that will be a fire to drive them to great achievement.
>
> There is a life work for all....Under God the thing burns as a passionate objective of a lifetime. [4]

The zeal of many people rises and falls like a barometer. One day they are hot as fire, and another day as cold as ice. This displeases God. He is disappointed with people who do not give their best to Him, who are lukewarm, and have lost their passion. Revelation 3:15-17 says,

> I know thy works, that thou art neither cold nor hot: I would thou wert cold or hot. So then because thou art lukewarm, and neither cold nor hot, I will spue thee out of my mouth. Because thou sayest, I am rich, and increased with goods, and have need of nothing; and

knowest not that thou art wretched, and miserable, and poor, and blind, and naked.

To be lukewarm is to be moderately warm, indifferent and not ardent. It is a place of death. To be ardent is to be hot, glowing, shining, passionate or fiery. This is what the Lord requires. Excuses will not be accepted from the Lord, only repentance will. He counseled the Ephesians to anoint their eyes with eyesalve that they might see, and also to repent.

May your eyes be opened to the possibilities that lie before you. God can transform you into a blazing torch of evangelism and a passionate prayer warrior that will shake kingdoms. John Knox was known for his ardent prayers and fervent cry of "Give me Scotland or I die." Someone has asked the question, "Where are the John Knox's of today?"

I am convinced there are passionate Christians today, but there needs to be more. The challenge is to not succumb to complacency. Do not let the knowledge of this computer age or streamlined organization and prestige replace the fervency of those that lived before us.

We are at war today: war for our children, war for our churches, war for our families, war for our generations, war against Satan and all for which he stands.

We need to have the passionate zeal that Winston Churchill had during World War II. Days immediately after Dunkirk, all seemed lost and the invasion of England loomed threateningly. Forty-seven warships had been sunk in the operations off Norway after Dunkirk. When the evacuation was completed, half the British destroyers were in for repairs and the Royal Air Force had lost forty percent of its bomber strength. They were without arms or equipment and had left over 50,000 vehicles in France.

Winston Churchill stirred a nation to action by his passionate speech. He thundered,

> We shall go to the end, we shall fight in France, we shall fight on the seas and oceans, we shall fight with growing confidence and growing strength in the air, we shall defend our Island whatever the cost may be. We shall fight on the landing grounds, we shall fight in the fields and in the streets. We shall fight in the hills; we shall never surrender, and even if, which I do not for a moment believe, this Island or a large part of it were subjugated and starving, then our Europe beyond the seas, armed and guarded by the British Fleet, would carry on the struggle, until, in God's good time, the New World, with all its power and might steps forth to the rescue and the liberation of the old.

Mr. Churchill made the people hear his throbbing heart of passion, zeal and faith. He refused to give up, even if it looked like they had lost. He stirred a fearful people into action and the flame of fire leaped from the lips of one man until it swept a nation to victory.

This is the time to come alive with desire and fire. There are so many things that need to be done, and so many people yet to be won to Christ. Get out of your rut and throw your excuses away. Dare to do something today. Apathy is the death of a nation or a people. There must be a cause worth fighting for; there must be something for which to live.

It is almost impossible to stop a person from doing something when he has a will or fire to do it. Francis Mouthelon, to whom was awarded the prize by the French Society of Artists for the loveliest painting in 1895, had no hands. He painted with exquisite skill by means of a wooden hand. He believed passionately he could do it, and he did.

Nancy Merki, stricken with polio at age ten, was forced to wear heavy braces, and later used crutches. Yet in four years she became a swimming champion. When President Roosevelt asked her how she had become the youngest champion despite infantile paralysis, she replied, "Well, I guess I just kept trying, Mr. President." At age 19 she emerged from the national swimming meet as national champion.

It was the passionate desire and zeal of Francis Mouthelon and Nancy Merki that pushed them on in spite of difficulties. Your passion must be bigger than your problem, larger than the enemy's taunts, and firmly settled in your brain, so that nothing can stop you.

Zeal is a good thing. It either provokes others or inspires them. The Apostle Paul wrote a letter to the Corinthians and commended them on their zeal. "For I know the forwardness of your mind, for which I boast of you to them of Macedonia, that Achaia was ready a year ago; and your zeal hath provoked many" (II Corinthians 9:2).

It was their zeal that stimulated and fired up all the other churches. Zeal and passion are contagious. What are *you* passing on to this generation?

"My good blade carves the casques of men,
My tough lance thrusteth sure,
My strength is as the strength of ten,
Because my heart is pure."

Tennyson in *Sir Galahad*

CHAPTER 6

GIVE YOUR BEST TO PURITY AND GREATNESS

Oliver Wendell Holmes wrote the following poem:

Build thee more stately mansions, oh my soul,
As the swift seasons roll!
Leave thy low-vaulted past!
Let each new temple, [be] nobler than the last. [1]

Greatness of soul is not found in the deceitful or the false, or in weak character. It is first formed by truth. Shakespeare wrote, “This above all: To thine own self be true, And it must follow as the night the day, Thou canst not then be false to any man." [2]

Jesus said the *pure in heart* would see God. If you want to see God you must seek to have a pure heart. Eyes are clouded by impurity, and guilty consciences are torture. Benjamin Franklin wrote,

> Let no pleasure tempt thee, no profit allure thee, no ambition corrupt thee, to do anything which thou knowest to be evil; so shalt thou always live jollily; for a good conscience is a continual Christmas. [3]

Defraud not yourself by allowing the baser things of life to enter into your soul. Protect your mind from evil as much as possible. Do not watch things that taint the soul. Do not read books that weaken your morals. Let not the filth of the world find an opening into your mind. Purity is to be desired more than gold. Guard it like Fort Knox.

Let not the floodgates of impurity, filthiness and evil sweep into your soul, mind and spirit, but keep them awakened by things of worth, beauty and noble purposes. Sink not to the level of a beast, but soar with eagle's wings to heights found only in the purity of Christ. Let His warmth of love touch your soul and keep you untainted from the evil of bitterness, lust, resentment, falseness, hatred and immorality.

Stand like a citadel pointing to the sky receiving strength from above and not from below. Let your very breath breathe with fervent desire to mirror Christ, to reflect the glory from another world. Keep yourself from evil and that which would cheat you from being a vessel of honor. You are the master of your soul; guard it well.

Do not settle for less. Be all that God created you to be. Do not only keep yourself from evil, but pursue high purposes and lofty dreams.

> Hold fast to dreams
> For if dreams die
> Life is a broken-winged bird
> That cannot fly.
> Hold fast to dreams
> For when dreams go
> Life is a barren field
> Frozen with snow.
>
> *Langston Hughes* [4]

Make your life count. Let it not be as a piece of driftwood washed upon the shores of life, but do something that will enrich another's life, and then your living will not have been in vain. Be strong, not weak and living an aimless life. Let the greatness of God's glory enter into your soul, that it may touch the soul of another human being. Live with aspirations and aim.

> In ordinary life a man who is unwatchful, wavering, unmanly, and weak, achieves nothing, gains neither respect nor confidence, and, if he does not become an absolute wreck, is still as nothing but a piece of driftwood floating aimlessly down the stream of life, and

> carried whithersoever chance currents may direct its course. Such a life accomplishes nothing for its possessor, and no one is helped or bettered by it. It may not be marked—probably it will not be—by any great crime or weakness, but its very barrenness and uselessness are crimes, and it simply cumbers the earth until its end is reached. [5]

Be a person of worth. Let your presence bring a breath of fresh air into the lives of those you meet. Seek to be a refreshing, inspiring and loving individual. Fix your thoughts on that which is good, for you will mirror your thoughts. Reach into the wealth of books and flood your soul with wisdom, inspiration and truth. Let your lips speak only that which will lift, challenge and inspire.

Henry Drummond wrote, "There are some men and women in whose company we are always at our best. All the best stops in our nature are drawn out by their association, and we find a music in our souls never there before." [6]

An unknown author wrote, "He who loves goodness, harbours angels, reveres reverence and lives with God."

Seek to be these kinds of people. Focus on eternal things, things of heavenly value, for if your eye is on the eternal, your opinions and actions will have a beauty which nothing else can rival. This is where greatness of soul originates. Live for something of value. Rise above the miserable norm, and soar into something exquisitely beautiful. Live not to please others on the basis of outward manifestation, but find yourself by pleasing God, and you will lift those who are around you to a higher level.

Psalm 24:3-5 substantiates that a pure heart is blessed of God.

> Who shall ascend into the hill of the Lord? or who shall stand in his holy place? He that hath clean hands, and a pure heart; who hath not lifted up his soul unto vanity, nor sworn deceitfully. He shall receive the blessing from the Lord, and righteousness from the God of his salvation.

> Many live for show, for display, fine clothes, just "clothes hangers."
>
> Many are living just for gold and wealth, just cash registers.
>
> Many live just for fleshly lusts. None are ultimately so unhappy. Nothing so surely puts out the eyes of the soul as sin.
>
> Many live decently but aimlessly, purposeless, without great objectives, apart from the great movements of his time; blinded by selfish indecision and fail to see life's great opportunities of service under the guidance of the Master.
>
> Why not live the Great life? Every life He has completely controlled has been supremely interesting, supremely useful and preciously beautiful! [7]

A life of greatness is not determined by possession of material things, but by what people are inside. Lift your eyes above the paltry temptations of the moment that would give temporary thrills, and seek to be true to the highest and noblest things. Get out of the rut of the mundane and discover that life is filled with many possibilities.

Someone once said, "Every moment trembles with possibilities; every hour is big with destiny." Do not let life destroy the possibilities that are waiting for you to grasp. Let the greatness of God fill your mind with determination, get up from your bed of self-pity and start marching to victory. No one can snuff out the light of your spirit. Conditions, circumstances, and black trials will do their best to destroy hope within you, but if you do not allow them to, they cannot do so.

Purity and greatness do not happen in a flash, but they are continuing processes. Every decision, moment and experience helps to mold the person of greatness. If you will look at those who have touched others with greatness of soul, you will see they were ever watchful and never unaware. While others slept, they were industrious, conscientious and fruitful. Longfellow said it well in the following poem:

The heights by great men reached and kept
Were not attained by sudden flight,
But they, while their companions slept,
Were toiling upward in the night.

"For anything worth having one must pay the price; and the price is always work, patience, love, self-sacrifice— no paper currency, no promises to pay, but the gold of real service."

John Burroughs

CHAPTER 7

GIVE YOUR BEST TO SERVICE

Maltbie D. Babcock wrote,

> Life is not for self-indulgence, but for self-devotion. When, instead of saying, "The world owes me a living," men shall say, "I owe the world a life," then the kingdom will come in power...All there is of me is God's estate, and I am His tenant and agent. On the day of our birth a new lease is signed. On the day of our death, accounts are closed...So live, that when thy summons comes to give an account of thy stewardship, it may be done with joy, and not with grief. [1]

Life is a cycle of service. He who serves best attains success, whether that service be humble or of great endeavor. Jesus said the thing that made a person great was to serve others. How you work for your employer, how you do your schoolwork, how you clean your house, how you perform the most menial task which involves serving others is considered important. Matthew 20:26-28 says,

> ...Whosoever will be great among you, let him be your minister [servant]; And whosoever will be chief among you, let him be your servant: Even as the Son of man came not to be ministered unto, but to minister, and to give his life a ransom for many.

The key is to put your life completely in the Master's hands and let Him give you a spirit of love and caring that will enable you to serve and minister to others. When you and the Lord connect, great things happen.

> The chisel cannot carve a noble statue, it is only cold, dead steel. Yet neither can the artist carve the statue without the chisel. When, however, the two are brought together, when the chisel lays itself in the hands of the sculptor, ready to be used by him, the beautiful work begins. We cannot do Christ's work—our hands are too clumsy for anything so delicate, so sacred; but when we put ourselves into the hands of Christ, his wisdom, his skill, and his gentleness flow through us, and the work is done. [2]

God does not want wealth or material things to be a substitute for self. Exodus 20:23-24 says,

> Ye shall not make with me gods of silver, neither shall ye make unto you gods of gold. An altar of earth thou shalt make unto me, and shalt sacrifice thereon thy burnt offerings, and thy peace offerings, thy sheep, and thine oxen: in all places where I record my name I will come unto thee and I will bless thee.

He said, "An altar of earth thou shalt make unto me." Mankind was formed in the beginning from the dust of the earth. God wants the body, mind and spirit of man to be sanctified as an altar unto Him. From that altar He desires sacrifices of praise, thanksgiving and service to be offered to Him. Thus, the mind, heart and will become the altar of submission and the body the sacrifice of service. We are to offer our bodies a living sacrifice, which is our reasonable service.

You never know the value of service you give to another.

> A doctor did not want to make a call on a particularly bad night, but he went through a pouring rain to the home of a poor laborer. His services saved the life of a small child. Years later the doctor said: "I never dreamed that in saving the life of that child on the farm hearth I was saving the life of the leader of England, Prime Minister David Lloyd-George." [3]

Give until you cannot give any more. Serve in a hundred different ways if you must or can, but do your best at what you are doing. The life you influence may be one that influences thousands. The service you invest in others will prove a great dividend in eternity.

Let your service be accomplished with enthusiasm. Throw your heart into life, and life will resurrect itself in your heart. You do not have to go through life full of dread, feeling dead inside. Paul instructed us to give 100% to whatever we do, because we are not doing only for ourselves and others, but unto the Lord. He is interested in how you do *everything!* "And whatsoever ye do, do it heartily, as to the Lord, and not unto men; Knowing that of the Lord ye shall receive the reward of the inheritance: for ye serve the Lord Christ" (Colossians 3:23-24).

> Science and industry are not God's competitors. They must never be elevated to where they become our graven images. They cannot take God's place. But properly conceived and used, they are expressions of his goodness. They are part of the way He today prepares a table before us and anoints our head with oil. Therefore, He is as interested in what we do at our workbench as in what we do in church. [4]

An unknown author wrote,

> If we are not certain, it may be because we are living at too low a level. If we live for pleasure or for money or for fame, the spiritual realities must of necessity be-

> come nebulous and vague...Gazing constantly into the trivial blinds the eyes to the splendor of the eternal, and working always for fading wreaths robs the heart of its belief in the crown of glory. God breathes assurance only into hearts which are open to Him. To those who give themselves wholeheartedly to the service of mankind through His spirit, He communicates not only peace and joy, but an unconquerable conviction that when work here is finished, to die is gain. [5]

This is the day to throw our heart into our work and do all things unto the Lord and to serve Him with gladness. Adopt the attitude of Charles Dickens who wrote,

> Whatever I have tried to do in life, I have tried with all my heart to do well; whatever I have devoted myself to, I have devoted myself to completely; in great aims and in small, I have always been thoroughly in earnest. [6]

What you are doing right now will determine your tomorrows. You do not just leap into something, but you prepare for it day by day. Everything is a preparation for something greater or lesser, depending on the preparation involved. The following poem demonstrates the concept of putting destiny into every minute:

> He came a little sooner than the other fellow did.
> He stayed a little longer than the other fellow would.
> He worked a little harder, And he talked a little less,

He was never really hurried, And he showed but little stress,
For every little movement, His efficiency expressed.
He saved a little money in a hundred little ways.
And banked a little extra when he got a little raise.
Of course, it's little wonder that he murmurs with a smile,
As his dividends come regular,
"Are the little things worth while?" [7]

Little moments make hours, hours make days, days make months, months make years, years make decades, decades make centuries. Each minute of time is important to what you are becoming and to what you are doing. A story is told about two brothers: Richard and Edmund Burke. One day after Edmund Burke finished giving a very powerful speech in the British Parliament, his brother Richard was found sitting in silence alone. A friend asked him what he was thinking.

He said, "I have been wondering how Ed has contrived to monopolize all the talent in our family. But then I remember that when the rest of us were doing nothing, he was always at work." But then the force of this story is increased by the fact that Richard always was considered by those who knew him best to be superior in natural talents to his brother.

My husband often quotes the following poem, which expresses the value of utilizing every minute:

I have only just a minute

Only sixty seconds in it,
Forced upon me, can't refuse it,
Didn't see it, didn't choose it.
But it's up to me to use it,
I must suffer if I lose it,
Give account if I abuse it,
Just a tiny little minute–
But eternity is in it.

Author unknown

As Martin Luther King Jr. left the world the following words, let me leave them with you:

> We are challenged on every hand to work untiringly to achieve excellence in our lifework. Not all men are called to specialized or professional jobs; even fewer rise to the heights of genius in the arts and sciences; many are called to be laborers in factories, field, and streets. But no work is insignificant. All labor that uplifts humanity has dignity and importance and should be undertaken with painstaking excellence. If a man is called to be a street sweeper, he should sweep even as Michelangelo painted, or Beethoven composed music, or Shakespeare wrote poetry. He should sweep streets so well that all the host of heaven and earth will pause to say, "Here lived a great street sweeper who did his job well."

"In this world it is not what we take up, but what we give up, that makes us rich."

Henry Ward Beecher

CHAPTER 8

GIVE YOUR BEST TO SACRIFICE

Entrance into God's kingdom is not by symphonies of music but by sacrifices. Jesus said, "If any man will come after me, let him deny himself, take up his cross daily, and follow me" (Luke 9:23). Jim Elliot, a martyr, said, "He is no fool who gives what he cannot keep, to gain what he cannot lose."

The abandonment of every selfish plan seems like an unreasonable proposition. The rich young ruler in the New Testament could not give up everything. Jesus was testing him when He said, "Go sell all that thou hast and give to the poor." Selfishness must be utterly abandoned and fought to the last in God's kingdom.

Selflessness is the higher road of living. The price is terrific, but the returns are beauty of life and character, and unspeakable gladness.

A thousand voices are calling us to take the low way: the way of lust, greed, self-seeking and self-indulgence. Then a voice from Romans 12:1 marches into our lives and compels us to greater sacrifice. "I beseech you therefore, brethren, by the mercies of God, that ye present your bodies a living sacrifice, holy, acceptable unto God, which is your reasonable service." "Acceptable unto God" suggests that we might not be acceptable to God as we are today, just as Cain's sacrifice was not acceptable to God. How could a person not be acceptable to God? A person would decide that by his measure of sacrifice.

Paul wrote in Romans 8:1, "There is therefore now no condemnation to them which are in Christ Jesus, who walk not after the flesh, but after the Spirit." After your initial salvation, you then choose whether your walk will bring condemnation or blessing by what direction you take. Paul did not say one must be perfect, but he instructed the Christian to walk after the things of the Spirit, which bring God's blessings. Christians must constantly die to the flesh so they might constantly know the power of His life. "For if ye live after the flesh, ye shall die: but if ye through the Spirit, do mortify the deeds of the body, ye shall live" (Romans 8:13).

Pye Smith, writing in the 1800's, explained that a sacrifice is the solemn infliction of death on a living creature. Paul spoke often of his dying to his fleshly will, and being made alive to the higher will of God. He said in I Corinthians 15:31, "I die daily."

Paul explained how a Christian can become a living sacrifice and pleasing unto the Lord. He said in Romans 12:2, "And be not conformed to this world: but be ye transformed by the renewing of your mind, that ye may prove what is that good, and acceptable, and perfect, will of God."

Whatever affects the mind is the important issue here. The mind is affected by what is seen by the eye, what is felt by the touch, what is heard by the ear, or received by any of the other senses. That is the reason the Bible puts emphasis upon meditating on the Word of God and upon prayer. Prayer brings into focus God's purity, presence and power. The soul is touched by the Spirit and renewed just as a battery is renewed by plugging it into the main source of power.

Conforming means to go along with whatever is presented. To not be conformed means to be separated from the normal flow of ideas, ways and customs. Instead of following the world's system, there is a walking after those things which are holy, godly and pure.

F.D. Huntington, D.D. wrote,

> It is no less than for a man to be brought to an entire resignation of his own will to the will of God, and to live in the offering up of his soul continually in the flames of love, as a whole burnt-offering. [1]

God's appointed way for the approach of men to Him has always been by sacrifice. The object of sacrifice was to awaken and maintain reverence for God, and express men's feelings towards Him.

The burnt offering was the oldest means by which communion with God was sought. Its Hebrew name means "an ascending." It showed a desire to do God's will and surrender to Him.

H.P. Liddon wrote decades ago, "Nothing is really lost by a life of sacrifice; every thing is lost by failure to obey God's call." Sacrifice is distinguished from other ordinances of worship in that it takes the form of the rendering to God of a material gift, or of self.

Anything worth anything will usually have sacrifice attached to it. This has been proven over and over down through the ages by those who have made a great contribution to the good of mankind. Florence Nightingale, who could have been content to be a wealthy social butterfly, felt a stirring in her heart to become a nurse. As she completed her training, the great Crimean war was on and thousands of English soldier boys were perishing for the want of attention. She said to herself, "Maybe I have come to the kingdom for such a time as this," and so she sat down and wrote to the surgeon general of the British army offering her services to go to the Crimea.

In the meantime the surgeon general had heard about Florence's training and wrote her asking for her services. Neither knew the other had written. Their letters crossed each other in the English Channel. Soon Florence was on her way to Crimea with 37 other trained nurses.

When that delicate, refined, cultured woman reached those terrible scenes, the army surgeons looked askance at her, thinking she could never adjust herself to those awful bloody conditions. "They did not know that a woman with an awakened soul can do anything. Presently she flashed out a brilliant suggestion and then another and another and soon they were aware that a master had arrived." The British government heard of her practical program for sparing the lives of those soldiers and gave orders to give her anything she needed. The place was transformed and thousands that were perishing were saved.

Her sacrifice knew no bounds. One night, long after time for her to retire, she found needy men at death's door. There had been a terrible battle. The beds were all full. The tables were even being used for the wounded. Some were even lying on the ground. As the surgeons came by they observed that a certain group had gangrenous wounds. They passed them by, thinking that their wounds were past help and so passed on to the men whose wounds were fresher. Florence found out that these men were left to die. So instead of resting, for it was way past midnight, she wrung hot packs out of sterilized water all the night through, so that when the surgeons came in the morning, to their surprise they found the wounds clean and ready for operations. By this thoughtful, sacrificing service most of these men's lives were saved.

She wrote in her diary, "I am thirty years of age, the age at which Christ began His mission. Now no more childish things, no more vain things. Now, Lord, let me think only of Thy will." [2]

Can her attitude fit into this slot of time? This is a generation that is interested in easy ways, easy money, pleasure, and soft beds of ease. They want the results of the best without paying the price for the best. There is a tendency to have a crossless society: no commitment, no sacrifice. "Give it to me easy, sugarcoat it, and make it snappy," is the cry. Long hours of labor, sweat or toil seem to be ignored. Do not let the emotions of a society that does not base its values upon God's Word dictate to you.

God still requires excellence. Lukewarmness makes Him vomit. Slipshod ways do not please Him, and half-heartedness makes Him sick, and will not be accepted or tolerated by Him. Many cry, "Just let me get by. Don't put me in a yoke. Just let me float. When I feel like doing something, I will, but don't challenge me to be consistent or disciplined."

The story has been told many times about the missionary who was walking along beside the Nile River and noticed a mother who had two children by her side. One was sickly and the other was whole. The custom and religion of that land required parents to throw their children to the crocodiles in the river to appease the gods. The missionary noticed that she took the healthy child in her arms and prepared to throw him into the river; whereupon he asked her why she did not throw the sickly one instead of the healthy one. She replied, "Because our god requires the best."

Our God, the only God, higher above the crocodiles, false gods and spiritual darkness, requires the best also. He not only requires it, He deserves it.

"Life is a leaf of paper white
Whereon each one of us may write
His word or two, and then comes night.
Greatly begin! though thou have time
But for a line, be that sublime,—
Not failure, but low aim, is crime."

James Russell Lowell

CHAPTER 9

GIVE YOUR BEST TO GROWTH

Grow at any cost. Stagnation distresses and produces irritability and boredom. First of all, it is important to grow spiritually. C.E. Macartney likened a Christian's growth to an airplane. He wrote,

> An airplane cannot back up. It dare not stand still. If it loses its momentum and forward drive, then it crashes. The only safety for the airplane is in its forward and upward motion. The only safe direction for the Christian to take is forward and upward. If he stops, or if he begins to slip and go backward, that moment he is in danger. [1]

Inner growth is imperative. Woodsmen report that, roughly estimated, the root spread of a tree equals the spread of its branches. The combined length of the roots of a large oak would total several hundred miles. A good root system serves two purposes in the tree's development: it functions as an anchor and collects moisture, without which the tree could not thrive.

Likewise, Christians must have that hidden anchor and moisture to survive, for growth in the Spirit and understanding of the Word solidifies and prepares them for battle.

It is also important to grow mentally, socially and emotionally. Seek always to have a big heart, to treat others right and to be the best you can be. James A. Garfield once said, "If wrinkles must be written upon our brows, let them not be written upon the heart. The spirit should never grow old." [2]

Seventy-five years ago a group of teachers in Kansas City prepared a series of ten characteristics, with self-examining questions on each, by which one could judge one's own fitness in regard to appearance, ability, and relationship to others. They are as follows:

Neatness: Are my habits of personal cleanliness the best? Do I dress suitably? Do I keep my personal effects orderly?

Broadmindedness: Am I ready to recognize worth in others? Have I respect for the opinions of others? Have I the ability to consider both sides of the question?

Courtesy: Do I try to manifest a real spirit of thoughtful, kindly helpfulness?

Dependability: Am I punctual in meeting all engagements and agreements? Am I trustworthy about meeting obligations to the best of my ability?

Loyalty: Have I a sense of responsibility for the welfare of the business with which I am connected? Do I make my personal interests secondary to my business interests? Have I a real respect for my occupation?

Cooperation: Have I an ability and willingness to work with others? Have I a real desire to be helpful in all situations?

Leadership: Have I the ability to plan and carry out the projects of various sorts? Have I the ability to win the allegiance and co-operation of others?

Honesty and Sincerity: Have I the strength to be honest, under all circumstances? Am I straightforward and unaffected?

Perseverance: Have I the ability to stay with a task until it is finished? Have I a tenacity of purpose, even against great odds?

Self-Control: Have I the ability to be the master of myself under trying circumstances? Have I the ability to be pleasant and considerate even though others are unfair and irritable? [3]

Growth in all the above areas is important. No man is an island. Paul wrote, "For none of us liveth to himself, and no man dieth to himself" (Romans 14:7). The mind must grow and expand also.

Seven instructions for the growing power of the mind are in an old book, *Quests and Conquest.* They are:

One: Keep the body fit. Power of thought depends upon a clear brain. A clear brain depends upon good blood. Good blood depends upon nourishing food, deep breathing and proper exercise.

Two: Think great thoughts. Dream great dreams of power, knowledge and service. Cultivate the reading habit. The Bible is a wealth of literature. Read it daily. It will be an intellectual tonic.

Three: Learn to love great books. Feed on master-pieces of literature.

Four: Embellish your life by memorizing great hymns, poems, and classic epigrams.

Five: Store the galleries of your mind with pictures of great lives and deeds of the great. Have your own "Hall of Fame." Study over and over the influences which made for greatness in their lives. Come up under the shadow of their loftiness of thought, nobility of character and the sublimity of their courage.

Six: Open your jewel casket of intellectual treasures to kindred spirits. Exchange with them wealth of thought. Couch it in the most beautiful language you can command.

Seven: Look to God for the intellectual and spiritual illumination which shall give you power to see and feel the majesty of truth, in great books. [4]

Maltbie D. Babcock once wrote,

> Our business in life is not to get ahead of other people, but to get ahead of ourselves, to break our own record, to outstrip our yesterdays, to bear our trials more beautifully that we ever dreamed we could. [5]

Do not give up your ideals no matter how tough life may get. President Coolidge once made the statement, "I believe in living up to the best that is in me. For to lower the standard is to give up the fight."

Growth in each life many times is determined by how time is spent. The art of economizing is invaluable. The men and women who do the greatest things do them not so much by gigantic efforts, but by the steady, unremitting toil, and by making even the minutes to count. A little done this hour, a little done another hour, year by year, brings much to pass. Most things of value are accomplished this way.

The biographer of George Stephenson tells us that the smallest fragments of his time were regarded by him as precious. Mr. Stephenson was called the Founder of Railways and built his own locomotive. He was also an inventor of many useful things.

Hugh Miller found time while pursuing his trade as a stone mason, not only to read and write, but to cultivate his unique style of writing, until he became one of the most brilliant authors of his day.

An unknown author wrote in the early 1900's the following:

> The small stones that fill up the crevices are almost as essential to the firm wall as the great stones; and so the wise use of spare time contributes not a little to the building up of a man's [or woman's] mind in good proportions, and with strength. If you really are sincerely anxious to do any good thing, you will find time, or make time for it, sooner or later, however engrossed with other employments. A failure to accomplish it can only prove the feebleness of your will, not that you lacked time for its execution. [6]

How are you growing? What are you becoming? Do some soul searching and ask yourself these questions that were written over 75 years ago.

ARE YOU?

Are you like a garden of flowers or a nettle patch?
Is your life a palace or a hovel?

Are you a producer of harmonies or a hurler of discords?

Are you a comforter or a disturber?

ARE YOU?

A grouch or a gleam?

A worker or a shirker?

A romance or a tragedy?

A joy or a sorrow?

A producer or a loafer?

Are you good for something or are you in the way?

ARE YOU?

A success or a failure?

Cherished or dreaded?

Static or dynamic?

Are you always kind, loving, and tender or cross, peevish, and harsh?

Is it harder or easier to be strong and good where you are?

Are you a producer, a booster, a lifter?

Do you make things worth while move?

Are you a block in the way of progress?

Are you a victim of drudgery or are you a chorister in life's music?

Do you whistle and sing or mope and grouch?

Is your life like alfalfa fields, orchards and meadows, or a desert waste?

Are you on lifting tides of a never failing enthusiasm, or a cowardly weakling driven before the storms of temptations?

Are you a live fish dashing upstream, or a floater?

Have you a wishbone or a backbone?

Does your language suggest a barn yard sewer or a rose garden?

Are you a ship barnacled with weakening habits, or an ocean liner, clean and strong for the high seas of success?

Is life so delicious that your mouth waters at the very thought of living, or are you getting so little out of life that the dark brown taste in your mouth has spread all over your face?

What a pity to be ugly, cheap, mean, and unhappy, when you can be beautiful, strong, winsome, and useful! [7]

"A Christian is a mind
through which Christ thinks;
A heart through which
Christ loves;
A voice through which
Christ speaks;
A hand through which
Christ helps."

Author Unknown

CHAPTER 10

GIVE YOUR BEST TO CONSECRATION

Jonathan Edwards wrote,

> I claim no right to myself, no right to this understanding, this will, these affections that are in me; neither do I have any right to this body or its members—no right to this tongue, to these hands, feet, ears or eyes.
>
> I have given myself clear away and not retained anything of my own. I have been to God this morning and told Him I have given myself wholly to Him. I take Him as my whole portion. His law is the constant rule of my obedience...I purpose to be absolutely His. [1]

The act of consecration is an act of the will. It is a voluntary surrender of the life to Christ. To consecrate is to make or declare holy, or set apart for the service and worship of God. It is to dedicate or devote oneself to the Lord. Consecration is an indispensable condition of holiness. It is showing that we belong to Christ and not to ourselves. The Lord is enthroned in our hearts and is master over all the forces of our moral and spiritual natures.

The people who have failed to consecrate their life to God are many. They are the ones who make a bad bargain when deciding to do their own thing and to not submit to the higher will of God.

Sometimes children see things clearer than adults. A Sunday School teacher asked if any scholar recollected an instance in Scripture of anyone making a bad bargain.

"I do," replied a boy. "Esau made a bad bargain when he sold his birthright for a mess of pottage."

A second said, "Judas made a bad bargain when he sold the Lord for thirty pieces of silver."

A third replied, "Ananias and Sapphira made a bad bargain when they sold their land and then told Peter a falsehood about it."

A fourth observed, "Our Lord tells us that he makes a bad bargain who, to gain the whole world, loses his own soul."

Everyone chooses whether they respect the Lord God enough to give Him their best in truthfulness, service and consecration. God will never force anyone against his will. You make your own bargain with the world, or you make a consecration to God. God is not looking for bargains. He

"Man is still responsible. He must turn the alloy of modern experience into the steel of mastery and character. His success lies not with the stars but with himself. He must carry on the fight of self-correction and discipline."

Frank Curtis Williams

CHAPTER 11

GIVE YOUR BEST TO DISCIPLINE

"We will not accept into membership anyone with any reservations whatsoever," declared Lenin, the founder of Russian communism. "We will not accept into our membership anyone unless he is an active, disciplined, working member in one of our organizations."

This was discipline for the wrong cause. However, it could well be written concerning the cause of the gospel of Jesus Christ. He requires the same dedication.

To discipline self is a choice. We must make a choice between the way of ease and the way of the cross. The struggle between the two comes to all.

We can never acquire any great capacity for joy or peace as long as we shrink from self-denial. Matthew Henry wrote, "The first lesson in Christ's school is self-denial."

Paul wrote in I Corinthians about a race.

> Know ye not that they which run in a race run all, but one receiveth the prize? So run, that ye may obtain. And every man that striveth for the mastery is temperate in all things. Now they do it to obtain a corruptible crown; but we an incorruptible. I therefore so run, not as uncertainly; so fight I, not as one that beateth the air. But I keep under my body, and bring it into subjection: lest that by any means, when I have preached to others, I myself should be a castaway (I Corinthians 9:24-27).

The June 19, 1983, issue of *Parade Magazine* included an article entitled, "The Price of Being the Best," written by Bud Greenspan. It contained the following excerpt:

> A high price is paid by U.S. athletes who strive for Olympic gold medals—to be recognized as the best there is. Most of us would deem the price too high, yet they are willing to pay it...The preparation and the sacrifices required of aspiring Olympians are made day in and day out, year in and year out. The discipline is monumental, ever-present and sometimes oppressive.

Greenspan told about several of the athletes that competed in the Olympics. Seventeen-year-old Julianne McNamara, who was entering the women's gymnastic competition at the 1984 Los Angeles Games, had to sacrifice much. In order to get the daily training she needed, McNamara had to live apart from her own family for three-and-a-half years. She said, "I missed my parents a lot. I'd call them and write them every day."

McNamara trained every day after school at Marina High in Huntington Beach, California. These were her words during that time period:

> I go to school in the morning, then I train from 1 p.m. to 6 p.m., Monday through Friday. I'm so tired at the end of the day that it's difficult to do homework and impossible to have a social life. Boyfriends will have to wait until after the 1984 Olympics.

McNamara talked about the financial sacrifice also. She said, "It's tough. Before I became world-class and was able to get some sponsors, my training used to cost my parents between $5,000 and $10,000 a year."

Greenspan ended his article with these words:

> But the feeling is the same for all of them as they enter the arena on the "day of days" when all their talent, dedication, and pride goes on the line for those short moments of competition. They all share the thoughts of the incomparable Jesse Owens before he

> stepped to the mark in the 100 meters at the 1936 Berlin Olympic Games.
>
> "This is it," said Owens. "A lifetime of training for just ten seconds..."

The grueling schedules, financial sacrifices, strained relationships, and daily rigid discipline that is part of aspiring Olympians is for a crown that is fleeting. They feel like the sacrifice is worth their moments of glory. Julianne McNamara also felt like the training would benefit her later in life. She said, "I believe that the discipline, hard work, organization and goal-orientation that are part of my life now will also help in my later life."

The Apostle Paul draws a parallel between a Christian and a runner in an important race, but the difference in the two rewards is great. The Olympian's reward is for a season, but the Christian's reward is for eternity. James wrote in James 1:12, "Blessed is the man that endureth temptation: for when he is tried, he shall receive the crown of life, which the Lord hath promised to them that love him."

Everything comes back to the greatest law of the Bible: to love the Lord God with all your heart, soul, mind and strength. This is discipline. This is the war between the law of God and the law of sin Paul spoke about in Romans 7:25. (The question is not whether you love the Lord, but whether your love will manifest itself in obedience to the higher law of God, and not the lower law of fleshly desires.)

There are four things Paul says a Christian must do to obtain the prize. They are:

1. Be temperate.
2. Run certainly.
3. Keep under the body.
4. Bring the body into subjection.

Let us examine these four actions. *Being temperate* means to "be moderate in the indulgence of the appetites or passions." It means also to "be self-controlled, restrained, and abstemious in the use of intoxicating liquors."

This means that there are fences that surround our emotions and passions, lines drawn that cannot be crossed and standards which must be maintained. Those fences, lines and standards are found in the Word of God. He builds the fences; we stay within them. He draws the lines; we must not cross over. He sets the standards for life; we follow them. They are not to restrict, but to liberate us into greater things.

God knows that immorality leads to death, disease and heartache, so He gives instruction to flee from it. This is a standard or way of life for the contender of the crown. He gives instructions on how to live, what to do and what not to do. He is your *trainer* for the big event, that of receiving your crown of life and living eternally with Him in glory.

To *run certainly* is to know where you are going, to have direction and to have a clear vision of the prize for which you are running. James 1:6,8 says, "For he that wavereth is like a wave of the sea driven with the wind and tossed. A double minded man is unstable in all his ways."

He is unsure about his objectives and is mixed up in his mind. There is no plan, no discipline or attainment, just an aimless, purposeless run. The uncertain participant does nothing more than shadow-box or play around. He punches the air but never makes contact with his opponent. He just beats the air, not his objective.

The next two actions, *keep under the body* and *bring it into subjection,* are often linked together. Scofield translates verse 27 like this: "I buffet my body, and lead it captive." There are two different actions happening here: keeping and bringing. Let us look at each of them separately.

Keeping under the body is accomplished by the human will being in alignment with God's will. *Keep* means "to conform one's habits or conduct to anything prescribed." It means "to behave, to abstain or refrain, to not let go from one's control." *Under* means "subject to the authority, guidance, or instruction of; controlled, limited, weighed upon or oppressed by, either physically or as by affliction, obligation, or the like."

Bring the body into subjection is the fourth thing Paul instructed the runner to do. *Bring* means "to cause to come, or come about." *Subjection* means "to be placed under the authority, dominion, control, or influence of another or of something else." Put the two together and it shows that there must be strong positive action on the part of the runner who desires the prize. There must be self-control and submission to that which is right, not only to that which feels good.

There is one point of relief in all this, the little word *into*. *Into* denotes that it is a process. It is taking someone from a point without, to a point within. Paul requires not the impossible, but relates the proper lifestyle of a Christian. It is attainable, a little here and a little there. This is what training for the Olympics is all about. It is a lifestyle that involves daily training, not one big splash, but consistent, rigorous demands on the runner, which develops and tones his body to win.

Charles B. Williams, author of *The New Testament: A Translation in the Language of the People*, translates verse 27 like this: "But I keep on beating and bruising my body and making it my slave." Richard Francis Weymouth, author of *The New Testament in Modern Speech,* also translates this verse, "I bruise my body and make it my slave."

Recently Dr. Ray Kloepper, a medical doctor and minister of the gospel, was in our city conducting a marriage seminar. While I was riding in the car with him and his wife, he made a statement which I will never forget. He said, "While in medical school, I had to operate according to my will and not my emotions. It was sheer willpower that took me through those grueling years of study."

Discipline involves the will. You must *set* your course and then *will* your body to follow you. If you followed your body all the time, you would sleep later than you should, indulge in enormous amounts of unhealthy food, and function according to the emotional feelings that were predominant at that particular time in your life.

Chuck Swindoll once made a statement on his daily radio program, *Insight for Living*. He said, "The more freedom there is, the more discipline there must be." He was referring to the difference between the law and grace. Under law there was much quicker punishment and more rigid rules. To some people grace means a relaxing of the laws or requirements of the Lord God. This is not so.

The words commitment, discipline and sacrifice are still written into God's conditions for His people. The difference between the dispensations of law and of grace is the fact that the responsibility rests more on each individual. People must now do for themselves what the priests did for them before grace. They now must take responsibility for their own actions, conduct and sins. It is their obligation, although it is a privilege, to go to Jesus and ask forgiveness. It is their duty to map out their race and follow it through. If they do not obey the guidelines and laws outlined in the Bible, they will eventually pay for it; whereas, in Old Testament times, there was quicker retribution for wrong doings.

Christian psychologist Dr. James Dobson wrote the following words in his book *dare to discipline,* after listing the benefits of discipline: "As might be expected, there is a price tag on these benefits: they require courage, consistency, conviction, diligence, and enthusiastic effort. In short, one must *dare to discipline*." [1]

I dare you to apply the concepts and principles set forth in this book. When you do, you will find happiness, peace and love, and you will enjoy success and financial freedom.

EPILOGUE

An unknown author wrote the following poem:

I've purchased a town lot in heaven
On the city not built with hand.
I'm sending material daily
To build in that happy land.

I want to send good material
That will stand the test of time.
So I'll not be disappointed
When I reach that home sublime.

Prayer is for the foundation.
Faith and love for the walls.
Good deeds for the reinforcement,
That will stand when the Saviour calls. [1]

Your actions today build for eternity, so build well. Give like you have never given before. Everything God made, gives:

God made the sun—it gives.
God made the moon—it gives.
God made the stars—they give.
God made the air—it gives.
God made the clouds—they give.
God made the earth—it gives.
God made the sea—it gives.
God made the trees—they give.
God made the plants—they give.
God made man—he...?

The choice is yours. Will you choose to give Him your best? Remember the old Chinese proverb: *The journey of a thousand miles begins with the first step.* So take that first step today and begin a new way of life. As you give your best, zest for life will return to you, and you will truly find LIFE.

NOTES

Introduction

[1] Dean C. Dutton, PhD., arr. & comp., *Quests and Conquests*, (Guthrie, OK: Live Service Publishing Co., 1923), #135.

[2] Joseph S. Johnson, comp., *A Field of Diamonds*, (Nashville, TN: Broadman Press, 1974), 175.

[3] Ibid., 10.

[4] Paul Lee Tan, ThD., *Encyclopedia of 7,700 Illustrations: Signs of the Times,* (Rockville, MD: 1979), #1670.

Author's Note

[1] Clinton T. Howell, ed., *Lines to Live By*, (Nashville, TN: Thomas Nelson Publishers, 1972), 109.

Chapter 1

[1] Tan, 1352.

[2] Howell, 174.

[3] Johnson, 11.

[4] Rev. W. Harvey Jellie, *The Preacher's Commentary on the Book of Leviticus-Numbers,* (Funk & Wagnals Co., New York, NY: n.d.), 101.

[5] Ibid., 263.

[6] Johnson, 72.

[7] Dutton, #1218.

Chapter 2

[1] Tan, 1037.

[2] James Hastings, *Dictionary of the Bible*, (New York, NY: Charles Scribner's Sons, 1909), 687.

[3] Mike and Lorna Wieteska, *Man With a Destiny: Bill Drost The Pentecost*, (Burlington, Ontario, Canada: Welch Publishing Co., Inc., 1983), 27.

[4] Johnson, 156.

[5] E. Herman, *Creative Prayer*, (London: James Clark Co., 1921), 35.

[6] Steven R. Mosley, *A Tale of Three Virtues*, (Questor Publishing, Inc., Sisters, OR: 1989), 241.

Chapter 3

[1] Johnson, 166.

[2] Ibid., 167.

[3] Wieteska, 74.

[4] Johnson, 95.

[5] Ibid., 96.

Chapter 4

[1] Johnson, 24.
[2] Tan, 186.
[3] Ibid.
[4] Ibid., 186-187.
[5] Ibid., 158, 192.
[6] Ibid., 157.
[7] Ibid., 184.
[8] Howell, 172.

Chapter 5

[1] Tan, 765.
[2] Ibid., 1669.
[3] Johnson, 71.
[4] Dutton, #590.

Chapter 6

[1] Dutton, #254.
[2] Ibid., #143-A.
[3] Howell, 30.
[4] Ibid., 36.
[5] Dutton, #176.
[6] Ibid., #1158-C.

[7] Ibid., #1288.

Chapter 7

[1] Dutton, #646.
[2] Johnson, 72.
[3] Ibid., 38.
[4] Ibid., 13.
[5] Dutton, #98.
[6] Ibid., #231.
[7] Ibid., #273-B.

Chapter 8

[1] Jellie, 101.
[2] Tan, 271.

Chapter 9

[1] Tan, 184.
[2] Dutton, #143-B.
[3] Ibid., #195.
[4] Howell, 36.
[5] Dutton, #229.
[6] Ibid., #426-B.
[7] Ibid., #1571.

Chapter 10

[1] Tan, 271.

[2] Johnson, 72.
[3] Ibid., 108.
[4] Tan, 1178.
[5] Howell, 156

Chapter 11

[1] James Dobson Ph.D., *dare to discipline,* (Wheaton, IL: Tyndale House Publishers, c. 1971), 14.

Epilogue

[1] Tan, 546.